"Around the Hill and A-Far-Away Off"

"Christmas at Grandmother's"

Written by: Marcus Fielding Hart
Illustrated by: Nicolle R. Murray

Dedicated to: "Grandmother"
Ann Eliza Doney Lowe (1863-1947)
and all her descendants

"Around the Hill and A-Far-Away Off"
Christmas at Grandmother's
Illustrated Edition
Poem written by Mark Hart
Text from Newly Revised Fourth Edition of "Apple Blossom Daze"
(c) 1960 and (c) 1985 Mark Hart Educational Service
Preston, ID 83263

Illustrations and book design by Nicolle R. Murray (c) 2025
Published by Capering Castles (c) 2025

Description: A delightful, bubbling narrative of a
young pre-World War I boy describing the joys, and festivities
of spending Christmas at his maternal grandmother's.

All rights Reserved

ISBN: 979-89926001-0-0

Preface

    I first read "Around the Hill and A-Far-Away Off/Christmas at Grandmother's" in 2018 when my mother-in-law, one of the daughters of Mark Hart, gifted us with a copy of his *"Apple Blossom Daze"*. Of all the fun, rambuctious stories in the book, this poem about spending Christmas at his grandmother's house particularly caught my fancy.

    I loved the rich pictures it conjured up in my head as I read it and felt it would be a fun project to illustrate. I also have two sons, great grandchildren of the author, whom I felt would probably enjoy a picture book rendering of their ancestor's story, especially as the poem centered on boys and their activities.

    As a historic work, I felt it imperative to research to maintain accuracy when illustrating. I wanted readers to hear the story but also to have an authentic view of that time period and of the people in it. Choosing the date to portray the story was tricky. Mark wrote the poem as an adult and didn't specify an age or time when this event took place. As I reviewed biographies and notes, it looked like visits to grandmother's house were frequent and common throughout his childhood. However, in the poem, Grandfather Lowe is mentioned as already passed, which gave me a starting point: He died June1905 when young Mark was just a year old.

    Digging deeper, I was lucky to find two pictures of Mark and four of his brothers and his father, taken in the summer of 1913. At the time of this photo he was eight years old, going on nine- a good approximate age for the timing of his poem, (judging by the activities they engaged in.) I eventually settled on the December of 1912 after investigating more into the next question: Who exactly was in Grandmother's Christmas party group?

    Back then large families were common, and Grandmother Lowe had 13 children before Grandfather Lowe passed away. Of Grandmother Lowe's 13 children, (at the time of December 1912), several were married. So, to 'keep things simple', I took the liberty in excluding all of Grandmother Lowe's married children and their families in this depiction. (Mark's mother Ada and her children excepted of course.) It would've been very difficult for me to draw so many people and keep the pictures from being too "busy". I convey my sincerest appologies to them and their descendants as I'm sure they visited their mother/grandmother quite faithfully until her death in 1947. Rhea and Lillie, though over the age of 20, were not married yet, so I kept them in the picture, since back then it wasn't common for women to leave home until they were married or if they did leave for a job, most singles would usually come home for Christmas every year if they could.

    So, with this reduction, I now had 10 people in Grandmother's household: Grandmother (age 49), Ada (31), Rhea (22), Lillie (20), Scott (18), Irel (16), Jennie (14), Nolan (12), Acel (10) and Glen (8). Still a sizeable amount of persons but as Mark rarely mentioned the girls his narrative, I figured it was doable.

    Next I investigated Mark's immediate family, to see whom was alive at that time and would most likely be at the festivities. In 1912 Ada (Mark's mother) had just delivered her 5th child (Joel) in November. So there was Arthur (11), Halo (9), Marcus (8), Reed (7) and Joel (1 month.). Perhaps it's the mother in me, I couldn't resist inserting Ada into some of the pictures at subtle moments, as a gentle reminder and a quiet nod of respect to her though she isn't mentioned in the poem. Including her in the Nativity scene was an unexpected idea, but I think worked well, for it gave me a chance to show Joel (who didn't get any appearances until that one picture) and I liked the tender, personal connection between a mother with her newborn next to Mother Mary and her own baby.

    So that gave me a total of 15 people to work with- a comfortably large number. Luckily there were pictures of Grandmother, Grandfather and their children (at different ages), plus the exterior of their home available, making it possible to try to depict them as close as possible to what they actually looked like. I was able to find a picture of the old Cherryville schoolhouse as well on an Idaho school archive website which was also lucky.

    I was unable to get a picture of the barn, interior rooms of the house, the milkhouse, and the woodshed, as the structures have long since been torn down, so there was no going 'onsite' to see them. I 'made do' with any available pictures of those structures during that time period that I could find. There were no records about the type, number or other information about the farm dogs, so I tried to select breeds that were used most often for ranching purposes.

Throughout the research process and planning out the individual pictures I had the sneaky feeling Mark was peering over my shoulder giving suggestions and observations. There was an element of 'boyish mischief' in my workroom as I planned out the scenes and expressions which was rather fun.

Another important thing to note about the text is Mark Hart wrote this poem using one of his favorite, and signature style writing methods; laying emphasis on certain words to teach vocabulary. You will notice there are occasional words in regular font, with a pronunciation and description at the bottom of the page. Mark was a well known advocate for improving children's literacy skills, and tried to introduce new words whenever he could.

I disagree with the practice of altering a creative's work without their permission, especially after they have passed away, so I replicated the original text and it's formatting as it was published in *"Apple Blossom Daze"*, including the emphasis on the vocabulary words and their meanings as Mark Hart wrote it. There was, however, some ambiguity about the poem's title. Inside the main body of the book *"Apple Blossom Daze"*, the poem begins with the header title *"Christmas at Grandmother's (Around the Hill and A-Far-Away Off)*, but the section introductory page, as well as the page headers on the left hand side are opposite with "Around the Hill and A-Far-Away Off" coming first. Uncertain which was the official sequence, thus the official title of the work, I did more searching around. In his autobiography, Mark mentioned he titled the work *"Around the Hill and A-Far-Away Off "* initially when he wrote it, but decided to make it the subtitle under *"Christmas at Grandmother's"* later. Due to this notation, and after a review of English rules for formatting (based off of his placement choices in his published work of *"Apple Blossom Daze"* I still came up with contradictory results about the title. (Titles of creative works are listed first on the upper left corners of published books, followed by subtitles, so he had printed *"Around the Hill and A-Far-Away Off"* as the title in this instance.) So, I concluded to stick with *"Around the Hill and A-Far-Away Off"* for the main title with *"Christmas at Grandmother's"* as the subtitle as it was the first squence originally. This original order I felt would have more interest to the general public as an unique title as there are many other stories currently that reference a 'Christmas at Grandmother's.' and I feared his book would get bypassed as 'redundant'.

I conclude this work hoping that Mark Hart, and his decendants, and any decendents of Grandmother Lowe will be pleased with this rendition of Mark's beloved poem. I hope such wonderful works like Mark's live on, as a jolly reminder that our forebears were very human; who loved and laughed, played and worked just like we do. And that Christmas is not about presents; but about family (immediate as well as worldwide) and our need to spend time together and celebrating the birth of Jesus Christ, our Savior and Redeemer.

Nicolle R. Murray
Illustrator
January 2025

*The flames tonight in the fireplace
Are murmuring softly and low
To the tune of the wind in the chimneybox
That presages new-fallen snow,
And I'm carried back in memory*

PRES' AGE (v) To foretell; to predict.

To the days when I was a boy,
When I sat around my grandmother's hearth
In a Christmastide of joy,
And heard the hearth logs hiss and sing
As the flames about them purled,

*And breathed the redolence that comes
From burning birch-bark curled;
And when the logs were glowing red
And cracked like a gatling gun,*

RED' O LENT (m) Giving off a pleasant odor; fragrant

Grandmother'd get the popcorn out
To start the evening of fun.
We boys would thread the popcorn strands,
With cranberries in between,

*While the girls would paste the paper links
In the chains of red and green;
Then together we'd deck the Christmas tree,
Add a star for a diadem,
And harmonize on "Silent Night,"
And "Town of Bethlehem."*

DI' A DEM (n) A crown; tiara

Then Grandmother'd tell about pioneer days,
How they dug sego bulbs from the hill,
And cleared off the brush and the cobblestones
From their homestead in Cherryville;

How Grandfather played for dances at night,
And drove his oxen by day,
But that had happened a long time ago,
Ere his fiddle had been laid away.

"He was one of the first in the countryside,
"And to him the best hats would doff,
"When he picked up his fiddle and started to play
"'Around the Hill and A-Far-Away Off."

"Play it on the harmonica, boys,
"And we'll sing a chorus or two."
And the boys would play in their merriest tones
the merriest tune they knew.

The big boys soon would be telling their tales
Of Indians and coyotes and bears
That would keep us kids with our mouths agape
On the very edge of our chairs;

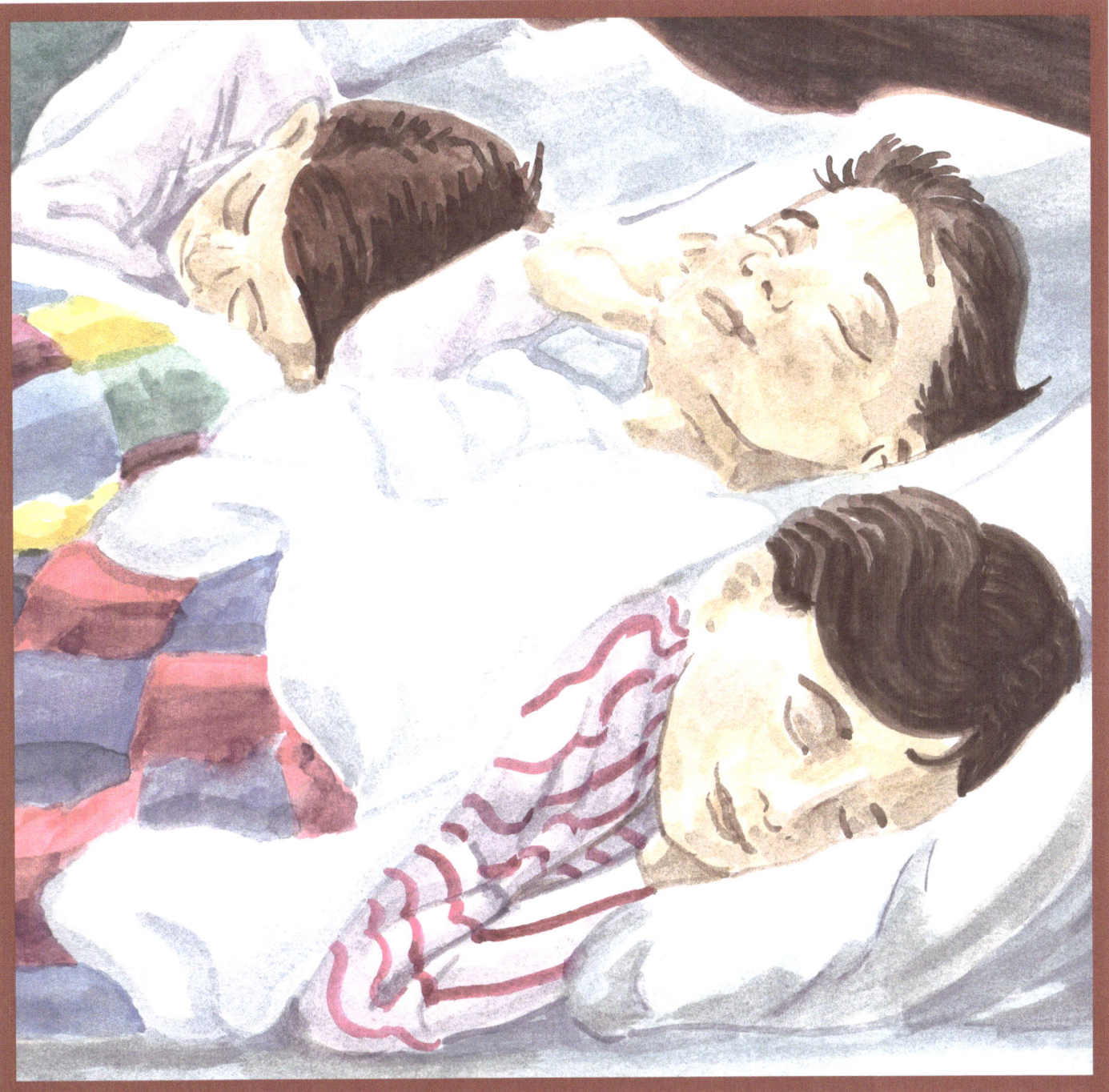

And after we'd eaten the buttered corn,
And were snuggled away in our beds,
You can easily guess the kind of dreams
That danced about in our heads;

*Then in the very dead of night,
When hardly a sound prevails,
A pack of coyotes might rend the air
With their uncanniest wails,*

UN CAN' NY (m) Weird; unearthly; not open to reasonable explanation.

Wails that would sally the ranch dogs forth,
Barking toward the hills
In a paroxysm of doggish bluff
That would fill our hearts with chills.

PAR' OX YSM (n) A sudden outburst of emotion; a fit of any kind.

And then when the clock was striking three
On the mantel hung with socks,
We'd fancy that jolly old St. Nick
Was stuck in the chimneybox.

Our sleep would be but a troubled dream,
The hours, miniature years,
Yet, morning would find us eager to go
As we'd hear the big boy's cheers;

We'd race to the windows in ecstasy,
And thrusting forth our heads,
We'd seen a garden of alabaster
On fences and trees and sheds.

EC' STA SY (n) A mystic trance; uncontrollable or excessive emotion.
AL' A BAS TER (n) A white, marblelike mineral.

One look at the world and we'd be dressed,
Then quietly down the stair,
We'd inch our way toward the living room,
For someone was sure to be there;

And when we'd arrive at the stair-way door,
The latch we'd silently lift,
To be the first, if luck were ours,
In shouting, "Christmas Gift!"

But Grandmother'd always be the first,
And she'd chuckle with joy to see
Us search for our gifts among the boughs
Of the bushy Christmas tree.

*There'd be skates and toys and candy and nuts
And sleds and mitts, if you please;
And soon we'd be kicking pristine trails
In snow that was up to our knees;*

PRIS' TINE (m) Pertaining to the earliest time or state.

The frisky dogs would cavort about,
Gulping the pearly dew,
Plowing trails with their flaky snouts,
As dogs are wont to do.

CA VORT' (v) To prance about, as a horse.

Then fox-and-geese would be the order of the day,
And we'd chase each other about,
Crossing the trails and re-crossing again,
Around and in and out;

*But soon the snowballs would be flying fast,
So we'd choose up sides to see
Who could blast the "foe" from the enemy forts
We had built in wildest glee;*

With sleds we'd climb to the top of a hill,
And after a trail had been made,
We'd measure its length like a skier in flight
And hardly a boy'd be afraid;

And then we'd saunter back to the yard
And make a giant snowman,
And dress him up with buttons and pipe
And a hat from an old milk can.

*Then Grandmother'd call us into the house,
When the banquet table was set
With the choicest foods that a boy ever saw,
To a feast that I'll never forget:*

Potatoes and gravy and turkey and rolls,
Choke cherry jelly and dressing,
Pudding and pie with cream an inch thick,
All from the harvest's rich blessing.

*And then after dinner we'd take up our guns
And head for the briar patch,
Where the cottontails were sure to be out
On their warren's snowy thatch;*

WAR' REN (n) A place where rabbits live and breed.

*And as we'd make our way through the gap
On trails that few hunters knew,
We'd see tiny prints and holes in the snow
That weasels had burrowed into;*

And here'd be a place where a covey of grouse
Had tracked about in the weeds,
Leaving the marks of their outstreched wings
Where they'd fluttered about for seeds.

Then we'd cross o'er the dam by the one-room school,
With woodpecker holes in the door,
And return to the ranch along Maple Creek,
Which was covered completely o'er,

Except where the water had sluiced around,
Cutting snow from the rocks and the bank,
Or tumbled down in a wild cataract
That gurgled and eddied and sank;

CAT' A RACT (n) A furious rush or downpour of water; a waterfall.
ED' DY (n) A small whirlpool.

But when a chill blast would sweep through the draw,
And a crust was beginning to form,
We'd quicken our pace and pull on our mitts
And make a bee-line for the barn;

For the wood must be got and the chips carried in,
The chickens and pigs must be fed;
So when we'd arrive at the giant woodpile
That stood by the side of the shed,

We'd load up our arms and fill up the bin,
While the big boys were feeding the stock,
And milking the cows and bedding them down
And taking account of the flock;

But ere they had finished their duties at night,
The lanterns would have to be lit;
And the shadows that straddled the fences and barns
Were eerie, I'll have to admit.

EE' RIE (m) Awe-inspiring; weird; stricken with fear.

Then when the boys would start for the house,
With lanterns and milkcans between,
There would be monstrosities striding about,
The likes of which seldom are seen;

MON STROS' I TY (n) Anything unnaturally huge, hideous, or deformed.

*But long before the big boys were through,
We'd eaten and skipped off to bed,
For we were exhausted, as well you may guess,
And after our prayers had been said,*

There'd come from the milkhouse a faint humming drone,
And listening closer we'd hear
The cream separator starting to wind
It's crescendo of somnolent cheer;

SOM' NO LENT (m) Inclined to sleep; drowsy; inducing sleepiness.

*And as it would climb to its apogee,
In a siren sort of a way,
We'd re-live the joys at Grandmother's place
On wonderful Christmas day.*

AP' O GEE (n) The highest or most distant point; the climax; culmination.

And we'd think of the Babe in the Manger,
and the Star over Bethlehem,
And the marvelous gift of eternal life
God proffers the children of men.

PROF' FER (v) To offer for acceptance; as, to proffer assistance.

*Then after the siren had faded away,
When from us there was hardly a cough,
We'd hear Grandmother's voice singing sweetly below,
"Around the Hill and A-Far-Away Off."*

About the Author

Marcus or 'Mark" Fielding Hart was born in Preston, Idaho, March 30, 1904 to Arthur William Hart and Ada Doney Lowe. The third of ten children, Mark grew up in a loving, hard working home. In his early years he excelled at spelling and poetry.

After graduating from Preston Highschool in 1924, he went on to obtain a Bachelor of Science in Arts and Sciences (a double major degree in English and Instrumental Music) from Utah State University, June 1, 1935 and a Masters of Education (major in Administrative Education with a minor in Philosophy of Education) at the University of Washington August 27, 1943.

He served three short term missions for the Church of Jesus Christ of Latterday Saints: Northern California; from June 4, 1929 to December 10, 1930, California Mission: June 3, 1930 to July 22, 1932, and Northwestern States Pacific Mission/Alaska; May 6, 1932 to August 1932.

He taught English and Instrumental Music for 21 years in Utah, Idaho, and Washington, and served two terms as Superintendent of Public Instruction for Franklin County Idaho Schools (1946-1950).

Mark also served two terms in the Idaho State Legislature; (1963-1964 and 1969-1970) first term as a Representative from Franklin County; then as a Representative of Bear Lake, Caribou, and Franklin Counties.

He became a member of Phi Delta Kappan in 1941 and contributed to state and national magazines, as well as to local magazines and newspapers. His written works include *"Apples of Gold"* (a poetry collection), *"Apple Blossom Daze"* (A collection of early personal life stories and poems) and, *"Marcus the Great"* (his autobiography). He also compiled *"Aerospace Word Power" for NASA* (1961) a science supplement tester and vocabulary builder for children. But Mark Hart is best known for his *"New Diacritic Word Power Testers and Builders"* (1950), one of America's first systematic approaches to programmed vocabulary building. Over a million and a half of these books have been sold throughout America and in several countires around the world.

He played both the violin and piano and enjoyed singing. His marching bands included The Hiawatha Junior High School Band, Hiawatha Utah (1932-1934), The Lava Hot Springs Highschool Band, Lava Hot Springs Idaho, (1934-1935) American Falls Highschool Band, American Falls Idaho, (1935-1937) Bothell Marching Band, Bothell Washington, (1937-1946) and Preston High School Band, Preston Idaho, (1946). His marching bands won scores of prizes, including first place and sweepstakes prizes in the Portland Rose Festival Parade, and special honors in the Pasadena Tournament of Roses parade.

Mark married Clara Walburger of Lethbridge, Alberta, Canada, August 26, 1933. They had nine children, and numerous branches of descendants following to date. After Clara's death (April 21, 1978) he married Lois Daines Griffeth, December 27, 1979, who later passed away December 6, 1992.

Mark Hart passed away December 30, 1994 in his hometown of Preston Idaho.

About the Illustrator

Nicolle Raty Murray was born in Salt Lake City, Utah to Dallas Laine Raty and Janae Kitchen in 1979. The third of six children, Nicolle's family moved extensively to various locations in the Western United States during their growing up years, eventually settling in Eastern Idaho.

Homeschooled from the 4th grade, Nicolle taught herself how to draw, is an avid reader, loves to create and research.

She graduated from homeschool in 1997 and went on to get an Associates Degree in the Arts from Ricks College April of 2000, and a Bachelor's Degree in Graphic Design and Illustration with a Minor in History from Brigham Young University June 2004.

She served a fulltime mission for the Church of Jesus Christ of Latterday Saints to Alberta, Canada; November 2000 to April 2002.

Nicolle's artistic skills extend to a broad range of mediums and applications. Foremost an illustrator she has illustrated over 20 books with genres in Young Adult Science Fiction and Fantasy, Adult Historical fiction, Adult Science Fiction and Fantasy, Religious, Children's Picture Books (Fiction and Non Fiction), and Coloring books.

Nicolle has also taught art classes, designed logos, marketing signage and 3D displays, created numerous fine art paintings and wall murals, created storyboard and character designs, designed and created toys for children, designed and painted Native American crafts and regalia, created cake 'paintings', and worked in landscape and home design. In 2012 she was awarded 1st Place in the Western Division for Home Depot's Veteran's Day Apron Decorating Contest.

Nicolle attended the Rocky Mountain College of Art and Design in Denver Colorado, pursuing an second Bachelor's Degree in Children's Book Illustration in but dropped out to marry Adam Murray in 2014. They have two living children and one stepchild (from Adam's first marriage).